WRITE RIGHT!

COMMAS AND COLONS
with Your Class

By Kristen Rajczak

Gareth Stevens
Publishing

Please visit our website, www.garethstevens.com. For a free color catalog of all our high-quality books, call toll free 1-800-542-2595 or fax 1-877-542-2596.

Library of Congress Cataloging-in-Publication Data

Rajczak, Kristen.
Commas and colons with your class / by Kristen Rajczak.
  p. cm. — (Write right)
Includes index.
ISBN 978-1-4339-9066-3 (pbk.)
ISBN 978-1-4339-9067-0 (6-pack)
ISBN 978-1-4339-9065-6 (library binding)
1. English language—Punctuation—Juvenile literature. 2. Comma—Juvenile literature. I. Rajczak, Kristen.
II. Title.
PE1450.R35 2014
428.2—d23

First Edition

Published in 2014 by
Gareth Stevens Publishing
111 East 14th Street, Suite 349
New York, NY 10003

Copyright © 2014 Gareth Stevens Publishing

Designer: Sarah Liddell
Editor: Kristen Rajczak

Photo credits: Cover, p. 1 Digital Vision/Thinkstock.com; p. 5 Darrin Henry/Shutterstock.com; p. 7 Sean Justice/Lifesize/Getty Images; p. 9 CREATISTA/Shutterstock.com; p. 11 Erik Isakson/Getty Images; p. 13 Jim Jordan Photography/Taxi/Getty Images; p. 15 Adie Bush/Photodisc/Getty Images; p. 17 Klaus Vedfelt/Riser/Getty Images; p. 19 Steve Debenport/E+/Getty Images; p. 21 Rainer Plendl/Shutterstock.com.

CPSIA compliance information: Batch #CS13GS: For further information contact Gareth Stevens, New York, New York at 1-800-542-2595.

CONTENTS

Words in the glossary appear in **bold** type the first time they are used in the text.

A LOOK AT COMMAS AND COLONS

Commas and colons are important punctuation marks. They make a sentence's meaning clearer. Depending on where a comma or colon is placed, it can even change what a sentence says!

Do you know what a comma looks like? A comma looks like a period with a tail. You can see a comma in yellow in the sentence above.

A colon looks like two periods stacked on top of one another. Colons are used less often than commas: they're still helpful in writing, though!

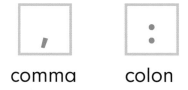

comma   colon

Commas and colons are punctuation marks you can use in your writing every day.

5

PUTTING IT TOGETHER

Commas are used to separate two independent clauses when they're joined by a **conjunction**. Each independent clause should be able to be read as a complete sentence by itself.

Paul had trouble with his math homework. He wanted to ask his teacher for extra time to do the problems, **but** he was worried she would say no. His friend Terrence gave him a few tips before class. Paul thanked Terrence, **and** he was able to finish in time!

ON THE WRITE TRACK

Commas are used to write about cities and states. Clara lives in Butte, Montana. Her mom was born in Memphis, Tennessee.

A complete sentence is one that has both a subject and verb. It can stand on its own.

FUN IN A SERIES

Items in a series, or list, are separated by commas. Commas are used when a series has three or more items.

Kendra's mom said she could **invite** a few girls from her class to a birthday party. It was going to be a sleepover! Kendra wanted to ask Denise, Tina, Laura, and Petra. They were all very excited. On the day of the party, Kendra's mom picked them up from school. They went bowling, watched movies, and ate lots of popcorn!

ON THE WRITE TRACK

Written-out dates use commas to separate the day and year. July 4, 1776, is a date that's important to the United States. A comma is placed after the year of a full date in the middle of sentence, as the example also shows.

Commas make sentences that list many things easier to read.

INTRODUCING...

Commas are used to set off introductory phrases and clauses. These often start with the words *while*, *after*, *as*, *although*, *because*, *if*, *since*, and *when*.

While the class was reading silently, the teacher began passing back spelling tests. The class had taken the test earlier in the week. **Because she was worried about her grade,** Lindsey quickly put the test in her bag. **After class,** she took out the test and saw she had gotten an A+!

ON THE WRITE TRACK

Do you want to write **dialogue**? You need commas to set off the quotes!
"I'm not happy today " Peter said. Suzie answered "Then I'll just have to cheer you up!"

Introduction words—such as well, yes, and however—should also be followed by a comma.

100% ☺ (A+)

NAME: Lindsey #2

SPELLING TEST - UNIT #D-3

1. excite
2. above
3. relate
4. canal
5. behave
6. remind
7. poster

CONTRAST, CONFUSE, CLARIFY

Writers use commas to separate phrases that show **contrast**.

Homework is important, but not always easy.

Commas help writers avoid **confusion**.

Without comma: Did the class lizard eat Mrs. Thompson?

With comma: Did the class lizard eat, Mrs. Thompson?

Commas surround unnecessary phrases. These phrases **clarify** something in the sentence or give more information. If a sentence is complete without the phrase, the phrase should be set off with commas.

Mark, who liked history class, used some cool pictures of ancient Greece in his project.

ON THE WRITE TRACK

When using two or more **adjectives** to talk about the same thing, use a comma to separate them. Frank was happy to walk home from school after a long, tiring football practice.

Without commas, you might write some funny things!

13

KNOW YOUR COLON!

While colons don't have as many different uses, they're still important. Think of the colon like an open door. It invites you to continue reading! The most important thing to remember is that a colon is only used after a complete sentence.

Colons separate two complete sentences when the second sentence explains the first one.

Barry handed in Matilda's Spanish homework: she had been out sick all week. Matilda wanted to thank him. When she went back to school, she brought him muffins: they were Barry's favorite treat!

Colons help you connect two related sentences.

15

LONG LISTS

Colons are used to introduce a list. They replace introductory words that could be used, such as *namely*, *for example*, and *that is*.

Carlo packs his school bag before he goes to bed at night. He doesn't want to forget anything. He has a lot to bring: homework, gym clothes, a silent-reading book, and his glasses. In the morning, Carlo has to remember other things: packing his lunch, taking out the trash, and eating breakfast. No wonder he gets his bag ready at night!

ON THE WRITE TRACK

Colons can be used to set off quotes, too! But they're more likely to be used when quoting a book, movie, or speech.

Notice how the lists following the colon in the examples on page 16 use commas between the items in a series.

IT'S IN THE DETAILS

Use colons before items of explanation or **detail**. It helps make your writing clearer and more interesting!

Most days, Genevieve has a big bowl of cereal and a piece of fruit for breakfast. But when she forgets, her favorite class changes from history to something else: lunch! Genevieve's mom often packs her favorite sandwich: peanut butter and banana. Some people in her class think it sounds gross. Genevieve looks forward to her sandwich's special features: the stickiness of the peanut butter and sweetness of the banana.

ON THE WRITE TRACK

Colons are used when time is written. Lunch begins at 12:15 p.m.

Using a colon helps draw attention to the detail following it.

19

LET'S USE COMMAS AND COLONS!

Can you spot all the commas and colons?

Patrick had to pick a piece of writing to learn about for his English essay, but he didn't know what to choose. He started with a list of ideas: Abraham Lincoln's Gettysburg Address, C. S. Lewis's *The Lion, the Witch, and the Wardrobe*, and the poem "The Walrus and the Carpenter" by Lewis Carroll.

After talking to a friend from class, who also wanted to write about the Gettysburg Address, Patrick decided. He chose his favorite poem: "The Walrus and the Carpenter."

COMMON USES OF COMMAS AND COLONS

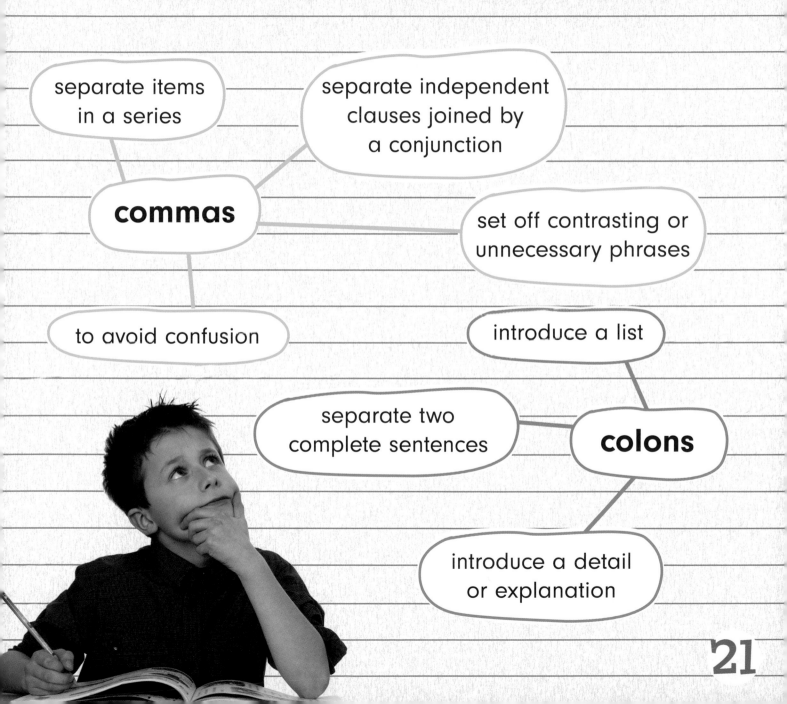

separate items in a series

separate independent clauses joined by a conjunction

commas

set off contrasting or unnecessary phrases

to avoid confusion

introduce a list

separate two complete sentences

colons

introduce a detail or explanation

21

GLOSSARY

adjective: a word that describes

clarify: to make clearer

confusion: state of not understanding

conjunction: a word that joins words, phrases, or sentences, such as *or*, *and*, or *but*

contrast: difference

detail: a small item

dialogue: a conversation in written form

invite: to ask someone to go somewhere or do something

FOR MORE INFORMATION

BOOKS

Ganeri, Anita. *Punctuation: Commas, Periods, and Quotation Marks.* Chicago, IL: Heinemann Library, 2012.

Lynette, Rachel. *Super Colon Saves the Day!* Mankato, MN: Child's World, 2012.

WEBSITES

Grammar Blast
www.eduplace.com/kids/hme/k_5/grammar/
Pick a grammar topic and earn points by taking a quiz about it.

Punctuation Practice
www.timeforkids.com/homework-helper/grammar-wizard/ punctuation-practice
Look over the rules for using commas and other punctuation marks, then take a quiz.

INDEX